SHEPHERDING
FROM A DISTANCE

DR. JESSE E. THOMAS

Xulon Press
2301 Lucien Way #415
Maitland, FL 32751
407.339.4217
www.xulonpress.com

Table of Contents

Chapter 1

What Just Happened?

One evening in January 2020, I was watching CNN as I always did in the past. The news anchor started talking about a possible virus outbreak that could have infected the food in the Huanan Seafood Wholesale Market in China. The news did not alarm me at first because it sounded like another virus infecting the food industry. In my mind, I was thinking, "We have been here before."

The news did not worry me until the latter part of the month. The media, doctors, and government officials started reporting that people were dying from this virus, which wasn't found in food. Instead, it was an airborne virus causing respiratory failure. Although I'm a man of great faith, my first reaction to this news was yearning to know more about what was happening. My wife and I grew significant concerns about what was happening because my children were born prematurely. The doctors always educated us on the severity of their prematurely developed lungs.

You could imagine the emotions both my wife and I had when we heard the news of what was transpiring. This virus seemed like it appeared out of nowhere and started affecting the respiratory system and causing death. The alarming thing was that people were dying in other countries, and the virus was killing people right here in the United States.

It appeared that this virus (as it was called at the time) caught everyone off guard. My wife was working for the local health department. She was briefed on a day-by-day basis about what was transpiring simply because no one could articulate or even comprehend what was occurring. Instead of resolving what was affecting our country and the world, we had governmental officials playing the blame game and deciding who was responsible for the outbreak. How I wish it were just that, an "outbreak," but that would soon change.

Everything came to a halt. The nation declared we were now in a pandemic. The death toll was rising, and we were required to alter our way of living and go from normalcy to a place of adjusting. It all happened so fast. Our son, who was studying at Liberty University, had to return home to finish his studies virtually. My wife had to pack up, leave her office, and telework from home. My daughter had to leave her school, teachers, and friends and return home to continue her education. I had to close our family business, "Thomas Boutique," and I was left wondering what was next for the church that I shepherd.

My family went from working, studying, and worshipping to simply asking the question, "What just happened?" I know we weren't the only family or individuals who asked that question in awe. When everything came to a halt, the community started to panic. Grocery stores had empty shelves, and local mom & pop businesses had to close or revamp their process.

Adjusting from normalcy became detrimental to the church because the church always reaps the repercussions anytime the community is affected. The church and community are one. Scripture shows us that believers are formed into a community that belongs together. Paul expressed this in Romans 12:5 when he said, "So it is with Christ's body. We are many parts of one body, and we all belong to each other." There is no way the community can be affected positively or negatively; the church is not involved.

Discerning Answers for Pastoring at a Distance

A shepherd lives with his sheep, and they spend many days and nights together. In a church, the pastor has the opportunity to shepherd his flock as highlighted by two keywords: *together* and *gather.*

In the New Testament, *together* is used over 100 times. *Gather, gathered,* and *gathering* is used over seventy times. It's clear that a church isn't a building; it's a people. The *ecclesia,* or church, is a gathering of saints or believers for worship, ministry, equipping, etc. Whenever two or more gather in the Lord's name, He is there. When Christians (sheep) come *together,* they are the church.

So, defining these words in English, we read …

Definition of gather:

gath·er | \ ˈga-thər *also* ˈge- \
gathered; gathering\ ˈgath-riŋ , ˈga-thə- \
Definition of *gather* for us, the church…
1: to bring together: to collect
2: to summon up, to prepare (oneself) by mustering the strength
3: to gain or regain control of *gathered* his wits
4: to conclude often intuitively from hints or through inferences
5: to draw about or close to something; i.e., "*gathering* her cloak about her"
6: to bring together different parts
7: to assemble

8: to grow or increase

Yes, all of these definitions of *together* and *gather* could describe what Christians in the church do. Yet, because of a pandemic, today's culture in America is sheltering in place, quarantining oneself, and socially distancing from one another.

- *How are we to be the church and gather together?*
- *How do pastors shepherd and care for sheep?*
- *Is it possible to shepherd at a distance and still gather together and be one in Christ Jesus?*

Some Biblical Parameters for Pastoring at a Distance

In 1 and 2 Timothy, Paul gives instructions to Timothy about how to pastor, shepherd, and nurture the flock of God, i.e., the family of God. The foundation for understanding what shepherding at a distance is about is found in Hebrews:

> *And let us consider one another in order to stir up love and good works, not forsaking the assembling of ourselves together, as is the manner of some, but exhorting one another, and so much the more as you see the day approaching.* (Heb. 10:24-25)

The purpose of being together, of gathering with others in the flock of God, consists of ...

- Stirring up love and good works in one another.
- Not abandoning one another or forgetting about others.
- Exhorting and encouraging one another.
- Increasing in doing all of the above as we are living in the last days.

As a pastor, I'm confident that gathering in worship brings God's people together. Assembling also brings God's Word, prayer, and songs to encourage the soul and kingdom fellowship.

At the foundation of pastoring at a distance is finding every way possible to communicate with each other for the purpose of ...

- Educating—teaching biblical truths for righteous living and making the right decisions.
- Equipping—one another with the training in righteousness to do ministry, good works among the saved and the unsaved.
- Encouraging—lifting one another up with faith, hope, and love.
- Exhorting—speaking the truth in love.
- Enabling—God's presence to be brought to those shut-in, sick, hospitalized, lonely, or lost.

**Pastoring at a distance is more than just
staying in touch with one another.
It is ministering to and serving one another
even as Christ the Servant serves us.**

As I faced this crisis in ministry and pastoring, I wanted to stay connected with everyone in the church and reach out to those in our community. There were times in which I had members of the church hospitalized during this pandemic, and the rules and regulations of the hospital were, "No outside visitors." Let me repeat this: absolutely, "No outside visitors."

Can you imagine how difficult and disappointing this was? I had to either communicate with the parishioners through phone calls or messages through the nursing stations. Hospitalization was a period of being isolated. We all know how the Enemy (Satan) can attack us at moments of isolation. Let's look at John chapter ten. Jesus gives an account of how important sheep are to their shepherds. Jesus states that He is the Protector and Caregiver of the sheep. Jesus exemplifies that we should have the same compassion for His sheep if we are to follow Him. Not being able to encourage and empower God's sheep in these moments (properly) was devasting to me.

I must admit, while the parishioners had isolated time to think, I did as well. The Adversary was doing just what Jesus said he would do; he was trying to kill, steal and destroy. The Enemy had me thinking, "What if they think pastor doesn't care about them?" What if they think I just didn't want to help? I struggled with how we as compassionate Christians could minister to those who might be sick or dying in isolation, completely alone and separated from family, friends, and other Christians. Henri Nouwen writes, "when two people have become present to each other, the waiting of one must be able to cross the narrow line between the living or dying of the other."[1] Now, I faced the reality that as a shepherd, I could face situations when I could not be present with another person when facing life or death circumstances. My heartache, anxiety, and pain were excruciating.

I desired to equip all of our members to do whatever they could to stay in love with God and others. Bridging the gap of physical distance could

---

[1]   https://www.goodreads.com/work/quotes/1202823-the-wounded-healer

be done in many ways, and together we needed to learn how. But such connecting and bridging the gap took more than the shallow types of relationships fostered on Facebook, Instagram, Twitter, and Zoom calls allowed.

We had to discover how to meaningfully gather together through many means and devices to meet all Christians' essential needs: *knit together in love*. My desire as a shepherding pastor, a servant-leader, was to have our church members' "hearts being encouraged, **being knit together in love**, and attaining to all riches of the full assurance of understanding, to the knowledge of the mystery of God, both of the Father and of Christ, in whom are hidden all the treasures of wisdom and knowledge" (Col. 2:2-3).

Journey with me as I discovered how to meet the challenges of shepherding at a distance. Join me as an essential member of the body of Christ, being ministered to and equipped to minister and serve others.

Chapter 2

"God, Please Hear Me."

Before I move forward, I think being informed of the church's history that I pastor will give you better insight. The Shiloh Baptist Church, which evolved in 1875, is the oldest African American Baptist Church in Accomack County. Shiloh Baptist Church is a member of the Eastern Shore Virginia Maryland Baptist Association and the Baptist General Convention of Virginia.

For 146 years, the church experienced leadership under thirteen pastors who effectively led the flock of disciples. Currently, I'm serving as the fourteenth pastor. I arrived on the first Sunday in December 2012. When I was installed as pastor, there were approximately twenty to thirty members who consistently attended church. From December 2012 up until January 24, 2021, we had over 200 consistent members attending church. There are approximately 350 members who are on the current roll.

Within membership, the types of employment opportunities vary, but the Tyson and Perdue Poultry plant employs eighty percent of the population. The balance of the congregation is employed as educators, technology workers, and workers in the healthcare industry.

Thom Rainer, the author of *Autopsy of a Deceased Church*,[2] said something that stuck with me. He commented that the church isn't healthily based on its quantity, but it depends on its quality. In other words, it's not about the number of people; it's the quality of people who make up the church. After almost nine years of pastoring, I was about to find that out.

Everything we have been doing concerning ministry up until the pandemic has been in person and face to face ministry. We didn't have any streaming services or broadcasts on the radio or television. This method of face to face ministry had been working for us. Still, now we were mandated by the government to withdraw from any in-person contact to control the spread of this deadly virus (COVID-19). After having a method that was working and being effective in ministry, I was now being pushed into a position to make a decision that would impact our church family. I came to where I needed God to show me what I didn't learn in Seminary.

Seminary couldn't prepare me for what was about to transpire. Suddenly, I found myself crying out to God, praying, "God, please hear me!"

God Answered with a Leadership Team

After much prayer and direction seeking from God, God gave me the blueprint to handle this crisis. I had been trying to do everything on my own, but God showed me that I had a great leadership team around me for a reason. I needed to trust them just as God had trusted me. I met with my team on a conference call. I informed them we had to shift from doing worship as usual and journey to unfamiliar territory.

---

[2] ThomRainer.com

Ministry isn't a one-person show.

Ministry requires a team comprised of servant-leaders.

Some church members may feel that the pastor is hired to do the ministry of the church. However, every minister leads and shepherds a congregation to understand that they are equipping the saints for the ministry.

> *And He Himself gave some to be apostles, some prophets, some evangelists, and some pastors and teachers, for the equipping of the saints for the work of ministry, for the edifying of the body of Christ, till we all come to the unity of the faith and of the knowledge of the Son of God, to a perfect man, to the measure of the stature of the fullness of Christ.* (Eph. 4:11-13)

"One-person shows" take us back to the day of Dudley Do-Right, rushing to rescue the damsel in distress. We may picture the Lone Ranger riding into the scene to beat up the bad guys and save the good guys.

Ministry is not about charismatic personalities wowing us with their sermons and television appearances. It's not about rescuers pulling churches out of messes and receiving the loving, lasting adoration of the rescued victims. We are in ministry **together**. A ministry team consists of the church with the Holy Spirit. Not me or any pastor bravely fighting the Enemy, praying, evangelizing, caring for the pastoral and counseling needs of the people, teaching, and preaching, can do it alone.

The sheep and the pastors are servant-leaders in the trenches of prayer, intercession, fasting, and spiritual discipline. The sheep and the pastors are witnessing, teaching, preaching, and discipling **together**. The operative word for ministry is **together**, not alone. The great Apostle Paul recognized his need to minister together with other believers ...

> *For I long to see you, that I may impart to you some spiritual gift, so that you may be established that is, that I may be encouraged **together** with you by the mutual faith both of you and me.* (Rom. 1:11-12)

We minister "with others," not "to others." The moment we see ourselves separated and alone is when we find ourselves discouraged, depressed, and deprived of the very gifts needed to do the work of the ministry. It's never me against them. As soldiers of Christ, we are equipped to battle against worldly enemies of the gospel, not one another. Our mindset is never "them and us;" it's *us together* for the sake of the gospel of Jesus Christ.

For the body is one and has many members, but all the members of that one body, being many, is Christ. By one Spirit we were all baptized into one body—whether Jews or Greeks, whether slaves or free—and have all been made to drink into one Spirit. For in fact, the body is not one member but many. (1 Cor. 12:12-14)

> **"Alone, we can do so little. Together we can do so much."** —Helen Keller

God Empowered Us to Shepherd Together to Continue in Ministry Even at a Distance

I've always preached that ministry doesn't operate around our convenience but on God's command. Having the church and community at heart, I gave the leadership team the blueprint God had placed in my heart, and we continued operating in faith.

One of the obstacles that we had to overcome was being in a rural area. There are many blessings of being in a rural area. Still, one of the burdens for us was that we didn't have good internet reception for streaming our worship services like other churches. We couldn't go on the radio and be effective with important announcements and other ministry updates with the membership of Shiloh. There was only one thing left to do to continue ministering effectively for our church family: implementing "Pull-Up Worship" services outside of the church in the parking lot. After evaluating the plan and the process, the team and I concluded that people would be safe in their vehicles. The musicians would be outside, social distancing, and I would be leading worship and preaching. I must say that when I presented the vision to the team, they were excited to make the idea become a reality.

Our last Sunday in the sanctuary was March 22, 2020. We decided to take ministry outside of the four walls. The following Sunday, March 29, 2020, were our first Pull-Up Worship services at 8:00 am and 10:00 am. We planned and prayed all week. We were astonished by the response and support of the church when the worship service began. I couldn't have started this transition by myself, and I had a phenomenal team to help with the process. The parking attendants, musicians, greeters, diaconate ministry, ambassadors, and finance team sacrificed their time, talents, and treasures.

I was worried about God hearing me, and God not only heard me, but He was preparing our leadership team and me. I found out that working together with our church members and those willing (and with the right spirit) to work together did more than I could imagine. Servant-leaders ministering to the whole church could accomplish more than just one person.

Here is What God Showed Me About Shepherding at a Distance

Pastors and people alike in the church exist to serve, not to be served. Our pastoral responsibility is fulfilled when we both lead like Christ and raise leaders--not followers! An effective leader equips believers to do the work of ministry (Eph. 4:11-16). John Maxwell in *The 21 Irrefutable Laws of Leaders* reminds us of this contrast:

Leaders Who Develop Followers vs. Leaders Who Develop Leaders

Need to be needed.	Want to be succeeded.
Focus on weakness.	Focus on strengths.
Develop the bottom 20 percent.	Develop the top 20 percent.
Treat their people the same for "fairness."	Treat their leaders as individuals for impact.
Hoard power.	Give power away.
Spend time with others.	Invest time in others.
Grow by addition.	Grow by multiplication.
Impact only people they touch personally.	They impact people beyond their own reach.

Servant leadership takes a page out of Jesus' teaching. Note Jesus' emphasis on servanthood. "Yet it shall not be so among you; but whoever desires to become great among you, let him be your servant" (Matt 20:26). Stop looking around for someone to serve and begin equipping others to serve Christ. People learn about ministry not so much through serving the "man or woman of God," but by serving "the least of these."

Your attitude should be the same as that of Christ Jesus, "Who, being in very nature, God did not consider equality with God something to be grasped, but made himself nothing, taking the very nature of a servant, being made in human likeness" (Phil. 2:5-7).

One of the greatest joys I have is serving. When I came to Shiloh Baptist Church as a pastor, I always wanted those serving to give the recipients a feeling of love and compassion. In fact, after less than a year, we adopted this motto in our discipleship orientation: "Committed to Christ and serving others with compassion." It's just that simple. We can't serve anyone with love and compassion until we are first committed to Christ.

Ask yourself...

How can I join with my pastor and the church leadership team to help them minister to others in our church?

What are some of the gifts and skills I must share with both my church and community?

Which of the attitudes that John Maxwell mentioned do I need to cultivate most in my church participation? Which do I need to eliminate?

Write a prayer seeking what God would have you do to become part of the servant-leadership team:

_____

_____

_____

Chapter 3

Being Creative

I remember reading a book Thom Rainer wrote in 2018[3] in which he asked the question, **"What is your church known for in the community?"**

The responses I read included, "My church is known for great preaching or for being friendly," "holding great events," and "having great things take place at their church." To me, they all seemed like breathtaking responses, especially when Thom Rainer pointed out that *all the reactions required the community to come to the church.*

Not all church participation and ministry happens within a church building!

I had to digest and understand that if these people didn't come to the church, they would never experience these highlighted moments. The sudden change of being in a different atmosphere gave the new impression of the church coming to the community instead of the community coming to the church.

---

[3] ThomRainer.com

For eleven months, we worshipped outside on the campus of the church. We were outside worshipping in the rain, wind, cold and hot weather, and even in snow flurries. The parishioners were in their cars while I was preaching through the different climates. Still, it was my passion and love for the gospel that kept me preaching, praying, and pushing week after week.

From March 2020 until January 2021, we thought we had everything under control--until we were hit with another blow. A severe snowstorm was coming to the area, and we now had no way to hold services. We needed a creative way to be more effective in reaching the church and community. Our team went to work and started researching an internet company that had just come to the area. They guaranteed us that their services would accommodate our requests.

January 24, 2021 was our last Sunday outside, and the following Sunday, January 31, was the introduction of our virtual services. We went from church inside the sanctuary, to church outside on the campus, to virtual church, and we have yet to miss a Sunday of worship, Word on Wednesday (Bible Study), and Tuesday Night Connection (Sunday School). All church meetings are now on Zoom and conference calls.

We now have a creative church by streaming on Facebook and YouTube and created an app to stay engaged with the church and community. While churches and leaders may have been against social media in the past, the statistics show that social media has played a significant role in many churches remaining open to this day. Adjusting suggests to us that being creative is just changing the method but keeping the message.

**Creative ministry brings us together and can change
the method while keeping the message.**

The greatest obstacle through this creative period was and is having to eulogize loved ones and not fully have the family in its entirety celebrate them as they wish. Graveside funerals and smaller funerals inside funeral chapels with a minimum capacity to say their farewells are heartbreaking. Not being able to visit those in the hospital and convalescent homes to bring hope and peace through prayer is horrifying to endure as a pastor.

The 5 C's of Creative Communication

The message we communicate in person, through social media, and through the internet must be Christ-centered, biblically grounded, and overflowing with the good news of God's love. Let's review how we communicate both to the saved and the lost.

How we share must be just right, or what we speak may not be heard or received by others. For example, I have sent text messages and emails to family, friends, and church members who misunderstood me because they misinterpreted my tone as being too abrupt, short, or uncaring. People read between the lines of what I wrote or heard the tone of what I said and were "turned off."

I have heard it said that 90 percent of all communication is non-verbal, i.e., body language, facial expression, tone of voice, etc. The same is true of written communication, the style and use of words that either communicate good news or bad news.

Creative Communication Cares. The scriptures tell us to encourage and pray for one another, and we are to accept one another as Christ accepts us. Caring communication listens to what the other person is saying and needs, and we must be quick to listen ...

So then, my beloved brethren, let every man be swift to
hear, slow to speak, slow to wrath; for the wrath of man
does not produce the righteousness of God. (Jm. 1:19-20)

Creative Communication Confronts. Paul writes in Ephesians that we should speak the truth in love, and confrontation can be assertive and affirming. One of the five love languages Gary Chapman writes about is communication. These "languages" describe how love is communicated through affirming words, physical touch, quality time, gift-giving, and acts of service.

I discovered that shepherding at a distance requires creative communication that is real and sometimes raw but never hateful, demeaning, cruel, or vengeful. St. Paul also said that even he, as an apostle, only had the right to build people up and not tear them down.

Remember that you can be right when you communicate without putting another person down. The cliché is that it's possible to hate the sin while still loving the person. Every type of love language can be misunderstood. For example, a hug could be misinterpreted as inappropriate physical touch, or a gift could be misinterpreted as affection that is not platonic. So, be sure that whenever you communicate face to face or at a distance that your words are carefully chosen and conveyed with the love of Christ.

but, speaking the truth in love, may grow up in all things
into Him who is the head — Christ — from whom the
whole body, joined and knit together by what every joint
supplies, according to the effective working by which every
part does its share, causes growth of the body for the edifying
of itself in love. (Eph. 4:15-16)

Creative Communication is Clear. Don't try to impress people with "big words" or "complex-compound" sentences. I was taught to preach so that even a child could understand what I was sharing. In I Corinthians 3, Paul said to the Christians at Corinth that he chose to speak to them as babes in Christ, giving them milk instead of solid food.

The clarity in all the different ways we communicate at a distance must be intentional and deliberate. We have to work at it. The Message Bible translates Proverbs 10:31-32 this way:

> *A good person's mouth is a clear fountain of wisdom; a foul mouth is a stagnant swamp. The speech of a good person clears the air; the words of the wicked pollute it.*

It's possible to be clear and direct instead of being obtuse and abstract. I invited a pastor to preach, and one of the church's deacons greeted the guest pastor after service. The deacon said, "Preacher, I knew your messages were scholarly and profound, but I simply didn't understand a word you were speaking."

Creative Communication is Consistent. Consistency is the exact opposite of contradictory. We can say something is a fact one day and say the exact opposite the next day or a week later. Being inconsistent fosters an atmosphere of distrust.

The Psalmist writes, "Everyone utters lies to his neighbor; with flattering lips and a double heart they speak" (Ps. 12:2). Some people say that political speech is like this. Some politicians tell different or opposite groups what they want to hear. They say one thing to one group and just the opposite to another group. Scripture calls this trying to please man instead of pleasing God. Being inconsistent in communication is simply lying. We excuse this as telling a "white lie." It's like telling a person you know who is constantly missing the mark that they are on the right path to success. Really? Although you may be trying to encourage the individual, you're still uttering lies to your neighbor.

Creative Communication is Constructive. The opposite of being constructive is being critical, negative, and speaking death instead of life. Proverbs 18:21 declares, "Death and life are in the power of the tongue, and those who love it will eat its fruit."

Before you speak to someone through verbal or written means, ask yourself, "Will what I say edify or discourage? Will I lift that person up or put that person down?" Remember, when we are slow to speak and quick to listen, we are more apt to think before we write or talk. At times when I say something wrong or hurtful, my wife will say, "What were you thinking?" In all actuality, I was reactive instead of proactive.

The Key to Creative Communication

It's difficult enough to have clear, consistent, confronting love. Constructive communication is following the example of Jesus. "*Then Jesus answered and said to them, 'Most assuredly, I say to you, the Son can do nothing of Himself, but what He sees the Father do; for whatever He does, the Son also does in like manner'*" (John 5:19). Simply put, only say what the Father would have you say, write, or do. If you can't do that, if you cannot speak life, then keep your mouth shut.

I had pastors who called me through this pandemic and mentioned they observed our creativeness and wanted to encourage me to keep moving forward. They ask a few questions to enhance their worship experience. So not only were we making an impact in our rural area with our creative ministry, but we were making a global impact.

Ask Yourself...

Who have you encouraged through creative communication?

What truth have you spoken that may have hurt someone's feelings, but it helped them live better?

In a setting, can you articulate in a way and reach a person with a GED and a Ph.D.?

What has your creative thinking produce?

How have you inspired others without drifting away from the truth?

Chapter 4

Was It Simply Cabin Fever?

That Sunday evening, the disciples were meeting behind locked doors because they feared the Jewish leaders. Suddenly, Jesus was standing there among them! "Peace be with you," he said. As he spoke, he showed them the wounds in his hands and his side. They were filled with joy when they saw the Lord! (John 20:19-20)

"A house is made of walls and beams.
But a home is built with Love and Dreams."
- William Arthur Ward[4]

After weeks of being quarantined, many can now identify that a house ...

- is a structure, but a home is a structure with stability.
- has a physical foundation, but a home has a foundation based on love and faith.

---

4   www.barrypopik.com

- is filled with all kinds of amenities, but a home is filled with an atmosphere of love.

If you're dwelling in a house, you must make a deliberate, committed, and conscious decision that it's time to shift your dwelling place into a home. Your home should be a sacred place.

Nobody should be able to disrupt or just come into your sacred place. It says in the article, "6 Ways to Create A Sacred Space At Home,"[5] clearing clutter is proven therapy for creating change in your life. Not only does it make a change in your life, but you never know what you might find when you start removing clutter in your space.

At times, if the space where you live is cluttered, it can be overwhelming to declutter. However, once you have cleared the old and unwanted clutter from your area and your life, you can begin to make room for something new. My ambition is to remove anything in my sacred space hindering me from receiving all God has for me.

Nosey people can clutter your life.
Back-biters can clutter your life.
Nay-sayers can clutter your life.
Negativity can also clutter your life.

Prepare for God's New Thing in Your Life

The word for *new* in Hebrew means *fresh*. Have you ever walked into a house that has been shut up and unlived in for months? The air is stale

---

[5] www.huffpost.com

and filled with mold and dust. You immediately rush to open the windows, let the fresh air blow through, and push out the old, musty, stale smells.

Our lives need the fresh wind of the Holy Spirit to renew us. We need the freshwater of God's cleansing and forgiving love to cleanse the sewage out of our hearts and minds. Instead of eating the stale, unsavory crumbs of the past, we need fresh bread from Heaven, from God's Word, to nourish our souls. We need God to restore, renew, and unclutter our thoughts. Memorize this promise from God and speak it out loud daily:

> *Behold, I will do a new thing,*
> *Now it shall spring forth;*
> *Shall you not know it?*
> *I will even make a road in the wilderness*
> *And rivers in the desert.*
> (Isa. 43:19)

I want to declare that the clutter in your life prevents you from receiving all that God has for you.

You should make these declarations:

- *I'm getting rid of the clutter in my life.*
- *I want what God has for me.*
- *I will work for, ask for, and earn the promotion.*
- *I want all my family saved.*
- *I need God to open a door for me to a new career.*
- *I'm grateful for my car, but I want new transportation.*
- *I'm thankful for where I live, but I want God to upgrade me.*
- *I'm hoping for God to do a new thing in my life.*

When Jesus rose from the dead, God interrupted history with a new thing for all our lives. Jesus had resurrected from the grave, and Mary ran to tell Peter and John that Jesus was no longer in the tomb. Peter and John go to see for themselves an empty tomb, and John outran Peter. John's Gospel says the beloved reached the tomb first.

- Matthew 28:1 reads, "Mary Magdalene and the other Mary."
- Mark 16:1 reports, "Mary Magdalene, Mary the mother of James, and Salome."
- Luke 24:10 says, "Mary Magdalene, Joanna, Mary the mother of James, and the others."

Assembling Together on Sunday Morning to Encounter God's New!

Although they may have different views on who showed up and how they showed up, one thing they all can agree on is that an empty tomb happened on Sunday morning. We assemble ourselves together on the first day of the week because Jesus rose early on a Sunday morning. I can't function unless I get my Sunday Morning Encounter.

The reality is, you would've lost your mind through this crisis if you couldn't get to your Sunday Morning Encounter. That's why it shouldn't matter if it's a virtual service or a pull-up service; you want your Sunday encounter.

After they saw an empty tomb, the Bible says the disciples went back home. How did the disciples are handle being stripped of what was normal to them?

First, John 20:19 says Sunday evening: the disciples were meeting and **waiting** for their following instructions. The disciples don't know what to expect, but they must wait. As you're reading this book, I want to suggest that waiting can be a tricky thing. If you're at a standstill in your life right now, waiting for God to move and work a miracle on your behalf, you're not by yourself when it comes to waiting.

- **Abraham** waited for a son.
- **Jacob** waited for Rachel.
- **Joseph** waited for freedom.
- **David** waited to become king.
- **Samson** waited for his strength to return.
- **Daniel** waited to be free from the lion's den.
- **The three Hebrew boys** waited for deliverance from the fiery furnace.
- **Mary** waited for the promising Messiah.
- **Jesus** waited for three days to get back up.

Waiting or being patient exemplifies that if you're waiting right now, don't worry; you have good company in the waiting room of life.

Secondly, the disciples are **worrying.** The Bible says the disciples are together with the doors locked in fear of the Jewish leaders. The disciples are terrified that their enemies will find them. Worrying and waiting is a terrible combination. You must choose which one you're going to do. When you start worrying, you're telling God "My circumstance is unchangeable." When you start worrying, you're telling God that what you're facing is impossible for Him to handle.

Jesus said, **"With man, all this is impossible, but with God, all things are possible."** Isaiah 43 reveals that the same God yesterday, today, and tomorrow is God of the now, the new, and the next. Right now, God has something new for you. New in your thinking, feelings, and your relationships, spiritual disciplines, your ministering, and your work. God wants to remove the clutter and obstacles from your past. Not only is God working on your past, but God wants to remove the worry and anxiety you have about your future. The God of the New desires to give you more than good ideas; He has workable, doable, and possible God ideas for your future. Will you let go and let God?

I've witnessed lives transformed, refreshed, and revived at our Pull-Up encounters. The freeness in the atmosphere was breathtaking. It seemed everyone was on one accord and simply wanted to get closer to God in the Christian walk. People of all ethnicities would ride by and just stop to listen to the services.

Many would pull over to give the church a monetary love offering. What was mind blowing to me was having more participation and seeing more people at our Pull-Up services outside than inside the church. The gratification was seeing lives changed and people being saved. I often ask myself the question, "What would've happened to those souls that came to Christ during our Pull-Up encounter if the church had closed during this pandemic?"

Ask Yourself...

When was the last time I experienced the Fresh Wind of the Holy Spirit?

Right down the obstacles and challenges that are hindering you from experiencing God in totality.

Am I willing to repent and release the vices that continue to block me from God?

How would my life change if I just told God "Yes"?

Chapter 5

Relationships & Responsibilities:
The Pulpit & The Pew

I believe some questions are being raised from the pulpit and the pew regarding their current relationship. Pastors may ask the question or even wonder if their members are even engaged enough to stay a member at the church. The pew may be wondering if the pastor is doing enough to keep them engaged. The reality is that both the pew and the pulpit have common and distinctive responsibilities.

I remember reading a post on social media that said, "The Devil would love to discourage and make pastors feel the need to compete for those under your ministry." The Devil will only achieve his goal of deceit and manipulation if the Pastor loses sight of their responsibilities. Competing with the next pastor in your area or network isn't taking responsibility. Taking responsibility is focusing on the sheep that God has placed in your pasture. The sad reality is that some of the sheep will stay, and some of the sheep will go. The church is a revolving door. Whether they are going out of the door or coming in the door, the opportunity to make a life-changing impact should never be taken for granted. No matter the situation, stay strong!

We can't ignore that both the pulpit and the pew have faced many challenges of uncertainty through this pandemic. One pastor in a setting asked a series of four questions from a pastor's perspective: How do you connect with the pew during a pandemic? How do you minister to families that are grieving and heartbroken? How do you encourage the parishioners to remain connected to a ministry that doesn't know what will happen next? How do you effectively disciple those that seem far away? These are all valid concerns and questions that any passionate pastor would ask, seeking to find the correct answers. The questions aren't the problem. What's problematic is having those in the pulpit without caring for those in the pew. Any ministry that isn't seeking positive growth is a ministry that has a death sentence.

Although pastors must find effective ways to stay engaged with the pew, it's also the pew's responsibility to remain in a relationship with the church. Communication in Webster's Dictionary is defined as information that is exchanged between individuals through a system. Informing the pew is the responsibility of the pulpit. The pulpit should inform the pew on vital information concerning the ministry. Merriam -Webster defines "conversation" in one definition as an oral exchange of sentiments between two or more people in which news and ideas are exchanged. Now, this is the responsibility of the pew. If the pulpit is communicating without having a conversation with the pew, how effective would the information and ideas be? The vision wouldn't go very far if both parties weren't on the same page. The pulpit and the pew need each other. Being on the same page is not just communication but having conversations, dialogue, and connections.

Let's review where we are now as the church and how we got here, particularly concerning the pandemic and its impact on the church and our community.

Covid-19 vs. Vaccination

Medical Doctor and Vice President Sherita Hill Golden of John Hopkins Medicine gave insight into coronavirus vaccines. She offered insight into what all ethnicities should know, especially people of color. One of the questions that the African American race raised concerning the COVID-19 vaccines was, "Can we trust the vaccine and the information about COVID-19?" In most states, statistics have it that the African American race leads in positive cases of COVID-19 and deaths. Although all ethnicities have been offered the vaccination, the African American race has been the most hesitant about receiving the vaccination. When asked why so many people of color are cautious about accepting the vaccination, the response was consistent: that they had their trust violated by the government in the past. So now, the government has the difficult task of rebuilding the trust of the African American race.

The broken trust between the African American race and the United States' government came from the Tuskegee Experiment conducted between 1932 and 1972. This experiment was conducted by the United States Public Health Service and the Centers for Disease Control and Prevention on a group of 400 African Americans abused through this syphilis study. One doctor explained that the purpose of the Tuskegee Syphilis Study was to observe the effects of the disease, whether treated or untreated. Statistics recorded that more than 100 men who were a part of the experiment were not informed of the nature, and some were purposely not treated and eventually died.

The United States government violated the trust of the African American race. They destroyed many black families who would have to live with infections, health complications, and death. Wives were infected, children died from birth complications, and many of the men died. You must understand that the Health Department and the government implemented this experiment. They bluntly deceived a group of people and violated their trust. The people who were a part of this experiment were told that the experiment was only to last for six months. Still, the Tuskegee Syphilis lasted for forty years. History highlights the African American culture's hesitancy to receive a vaccination that seems to be a repeat of history implemented by the Public Health Department and backed by the government. I think we can all agree that this forty-year experiment was a major violation of ethical standards and trust.

The Public Health Department (PHD) reached out to many of the Clergy, especially in the African American culture, concerning them receiving the COVID-19 vaccination. Being a voice of the church and the community, I believe the (PHD) started reaching out to the Clergy so they could bridge the gap of trust and distrust. At first, I was hesitant due to the history between my culture and the government, but I had to rely on my faith and dismiss fear. I made an appointment, and then I received my vaccination. I witnessed too many people die from COVID-19 that I knew, and it seemed like it was getting close to home. I watched pastors die, leaving behind their families and churches. I had family members that were infected with COVID and had to fight to survive. A decision had to be made, and I had to decide for my home and the church. I prayed for God's peace, power, and protection.

I remember one church conference call we had. A question that was asked concerning my perspective on being vaccinated. I didn't want to be opinionated. I didn't want anyone to feel inferior because of their personal decision to receive the vaccination or reject it. I was honest and transparent not only with those on the conference call but also with my church. My perspective is the same today as it was then. I believe that being vaccinated or not is totally up to the individual and their faith. A person shouldn't make anyone feel a particular manner because of a difference of choice. As leaders of God's church and community, we help direct the sheep, not become dictators of the sheep. So how is that accomplished in this divisive and turbulent time?

Chapter 6

Will Normalcy Return?

A statement says, "Historic recurrence is the repetition of similar events in history." In 1918, if you do your research, you will find the history of the Spanish Flu. This outbreak, this strain of virus-like COVID-19, killed both the young and the old. History records that this virus first started in Spain but made its way to the United States. When it arrived here in the United States, the country had to shut down immediately. Restaurants, theaters, schools, and amusement parks had to close. Although facilities had to close and revamp, it was challenging to witness the church's moment to close because of the Spanish Flu. I know conventions and conferences are canceling now because of COVID-19.

Look at the church. We have revivals, events, and annual days that are being rescheduled. If we look back in history, we will see that this isn't the first time this country and the church had to adjust because of a pandemic. The Church of God in Christ (COGIC) canceled their "1918 Holy Convocation" due to the Spanish Flu Pandemic. So, 2020 and 2021 aren't the first time that living adjustments have had to be made. The Spanish Flu, that had 500 million confirmed cases, had people living through challenges and chaos.

It's documented that the Spanish Flu in 1918 killed between 17–50 million people. There isn't any record of the first outbreak of the Spanish Virus that had people in fear and panic. Just like COVID-19, the Spanish Virus had people not wanting to be touched. Let's fast forward and see that we are over 100 years later, facing another pandemic. We've been challenged with the same fear of being infected by this virus as with the Spanish Flu. Let me empower you. The same God that was in control in 1918 is the same God that is in power today!

Commitment in a Crisis

In *7 Secrets to Success* by Matt Morris, commitment is defined as "the act of transforming a promise into a reality." This explains why we see so many people not enthused by commitments; it's because they can't see their promise becoming a reality. Obstacles, setbacks, and challenges can hinder us all from being faithful to our commitments. I've experienced that having someone hold you accountable to any task will hold that individual to a more substantial commitment. This happened with our church and community when we worked together during the COVID crisis.

Every Saturday for months, our church would partner with the community in having food drives that distributed food to families that needed assistance. When the people arrived to receive their food, we didn't ask them their church affiliation, and we didn't ask them their marital status. Neither race nor denomination played a factor in receiving assistance. The only requirement we had was to show up. We knew that serving others was the blueprint that Jesus instructed us to use.

In Matthew 25:34-40, Jesus gives excellent instruction on how important it is to help those in need. This showed the relationship of being obedient to the will of God. Jesus says, "Then the righteous ones will reply, Lord, when did we ever see you hungry and feed you? Or thirsty and give you something to drink? Or a stranger and show you hospitality? Or naked and give you clothing? When did we ever see you sick or in prison and visit you?" And the King will say, "I tell you the truth, when you did it to one of the least of these my brothers and sisters, you were doing it to me!" This exemplifies that when we are committed to doing the will of God, our service should always resemble the actions of Christ. We are the visible representation of an invisible God. So, when the community witnesses our service, they get a picture of who God is.

As the pastor of Shiloh Baptist Church, it gave me great joy to see the church and community as a whole working together in unity. The newspaper and news station gave the ministry highlights on making a difference in a crisis. We did food drives, toy drives, and clothing drives to not only assist those in need but also to bring a sense of hope to people's lives. We didn't take any credit for serving the community. All adoration belongs to God.

We haven't stopped partnering with our community. Partnering together demonstrates that commitment is more substantial when you have a group willing to work together. In the words of Luther Seminary, "Change happens best when it's experienced together."

As we move into the next chapter, I want to address these two essential questions.

- *As a church moving forward in witness and ministry, how will we communicate, dialogue, and continue to adapt to changes as our culture struggles to fight the pandemic?*
- *As a church, how will we engage the community in working with us to minister to and care for people as Jesus says, "As you do it to the least of these, you do it to me" (Matt. 25)?*

Chapter 7

Cultivate the Ability to Adapt and Change Amidst Crisis

Before COVID-19, what we called normalcy in many ways had become habitual, comfortable, and even "stuck in a rut." What I have written throughout these pages is a narrative of how we had to move out of our routines and into new ways to gather, worship, disciple, pray, evangelize, and serve our community. As a body, we had to commit to Christ and commit to each other.

In this concluding chapter, I want to help you recognize and learn how to overcome obstacles to change inside individuals and groups. Secondly, I will equip you to understand the biblical laws of change and put them into practice.

Recognizing and Overcoming Obstacles to Change

In Dr. Katy Milkman's bestselling book, *How to Change,* she identifies obstacles to change. Let's explore these:

1. **Impulsivity** – In addressing the need to change, we need to be proactive and not reactive or impulsive when planning what to do,

when to do it, and how to change. Impulsivity pushes us further back and towards failure.

2. **Procrastination** – Knowing that we need to change but continually putting it off leads us down the road to hurting or losing people in our congregation.

3. **Forgetfulness** – This often happens when we are trying to do too much all at once. We pile our plates too high, and stuff starts dropping off. We overcommit and underdeliver.

4. **Laziness** – We need to get off the couch, stop zoning on social media, set aside wasting time on entertaining, and begin doing what's productive, meaningful, and impactful.

5. **Confidence** – One-way confidence is an obstacle to change is when we are being overconfident. At times, we have lots of knowledge but not practical experience. Another way confidence can be an obstacle is by lacking it.

6. **Conformity** – When we try to fit in and please others, we are unwilling to change because we want to have the approval and acceptance of others.

The scriptures give us some guidance in how to change in ways that please God while producing good works that glorify Him and make a positive difference in the lives of others. Paul writes, "For we are His workmanship, created in Christ Jesus for good works, which God prepared beforehand that we should walk in them" (Eph. 2:10). As we become constructive in crisis and productive and proactive instead of reactive, we partner with other Christians who want to implement God's ideas and not just stay busy.

Ten Laws or Principles for Change

> *Do not remember the former things,*
> *Nor consider the things of old.*
> *Behold, I will do a new [cadash] thing,*
> *Now it shall spring forth;*
> *Shall you not know it?*
> *I will even make a road in the wilderness*
> *And rivers in the desert.*
> (Isa. 43:18-19)

The Hebrew word *cadash* means new, fresh, and changed from something old to something new, i.e., a new song or spirit, freshwater, or bread. Remember that God's mercies are new every morning. So there are ten laws for change--ten practical principles we can apply for adapting as we shepherd from a distance.

-1-

Change **Means that to Do Something New You Must Let Go of Something Old.**

Don't camp out in the past! To paraphrase Isaiah 43, *Forget [don't obsess over; mull over and over again] the past* ... Never let the past determine your future; God is your confidence ... your future. *Stop dwelling in what's happened; plan, process, and proceed toward God's future.*

In a memorable Sesame Street scene, Ernie is getting advice from the wise owl. Ernie is trying to learn how to play the saxophone. The Owl hoots to Ernie: "You gotta put down the duckie if you wanna play the Saxophone." Think of all the duckies in your life you are holding onto, such as past fears, frustrations, and failures. Let go of your duckies!

-2-

Change Will Cost You Time, Money, and Relationships.

Change is always costly, and it takes time to plan and to work the plan. Of course, change requires money to build something new ... change counts the cost. Jesus exhorts us, "For which of you, intending to build a tower, does not sit down first and count the cost, whether he has enough to finish it" (Luke 14:28).

Another cost of change involves losing some relationships. Some people will not go with you on a new plan, path, or purpose to produce the good works that God has for the church.

-3-

Change Requires a New Perspective, Plan, Process, and People.

Remember that we are new creations in Christ. God will use renewed people and new people to partner together to accomplish what He wants, not what we want.

Change isn't just shifting the old stuff around or merely changing lanes. It requires making a right turn and going a new way. The pain of the past cannot go with us. Bad and sinful habits need repentance. We must get over it, get beyond it, and then get it right.

We are getting beyond just treading water and maintaining the "way it's always been." Some churches are just trying to exist and survive the crisis, and we need to push through and breakthrough into the fullness of new life in Christ Jesus.

Change doesn't require insurrection or rebellion against the sacred traditions of our faith. Change does require that we are set free from bad or ineffective habits and that we step into the new process for transformation that the Spirit works out in us and through us. God's perspective and mindset are this:

> *For My thoughts are not your thoughts,*
> *Nor are your ways My ways," says the LORD.*
> *"For as the heavens are higher than the earth,*
> *So are My ways higher than your ways,*
> *And My thoughts than your thoughts.*
> *(Isa. 55:8-9)*

-4-

Change Requires Focus.

Who or what is your focus? Shepherding at a distance continues the same focus of our faith.

> *Therefore, since we are surrounded by such a great cloud of witnesses,*
> *let us throw off everything that hinders*
> *and the sin that so easily entangles,*
> *and let us run with perseverance the race marked out for us.*

*Let us **fix** [FOCUS]our eyes on Jesus,*
the author and perfecter of our faith,
who for the joy set before him endured the cross,
scorning its shame, and sat down
at the right hand of the throne of God.
(Heb. 11:1-2)

The focus must always be on the shepherd of our souls, not the under-shepherd or pastor of the church. Paul reminds us that people are to follow his example as he follows Christ. The pastor leads by example as a servant-leader with all eyes fixed on Jesus.

-5-

Change Precipitates a Fight!

Will we fight through any and every crisis, or will we turn and flee? Ephesians 6:10-13 reads ...

Finally, be strong in the Lord and in his mighty power.
Put on the full armor of God
so that you can take your stand against the devil's schemes.
For our struggle is not against flesh and blood,
but against the rulers, against the authorities,
against the powers of this dark world and
against the spiritual forces of evil in the heavenly realms.
Therefore put on the full armor of God,
so that when the day of evil comes,
you may be able to stand your ground,
and after you have done everything, to stand.

Yes, we face evil days of the pandemic, racial prejudice, strife, political turmoil, weather disasters, raging fires, earthquakes, floods, wars, and rumors of wars. We could well be experiencing the birth pangs of the last days. Disasters created by nature or evil people will not defeat or destroy us. We will pray without ceasing, give thanks in all things, and always rejoice. (1 Thes. 5:16-18)

-6-

Change Requires Follow-Through and Finishing the Job!

Yes, we may need to go where we have never been; do what we've never done, and even risk more than we have ever imagined to achieve the impossible and to prosper beyond our most incredible imaginations. We must ...

> **Focus, Fight, Finish!**
> *I have fought the good fight,*
> *I have finished the race,*
> *I have kept the faith.*
> *(2 Tim. 4:7-8)*

Decide to **<u>finish strong!</u>** "Remember that in a race, everyone runs, but only one person gets the prize. You also must run in such a way that you will win. All athletes practice strict self-control. They do it to win a prize that will fade away, but we do it for an eternal prize. So I run straight to the goal with purpose in every step" (1 Cor 9:24-26)

So ... to paraphrase Hunter Thompson:

> *Life is not a journey to the grave with the intention of*
> *arriving safely*

in a pretty and well-preserved body.
But rather, to skid in broadside,
Thoroughly used up,
Totally worn out.
Wow, what a ride!

In covenant with Christ and others, live life to the max!

-7-

Change **Involves Others.**

Remember that pastor is not a *one-person show*. Together as a team, we are accomplishing much for the kingdom of God. We must commit to one another that we will change. The church members work together as a body, all ministering to and serving one another as we serve Christ (1 Cor. 12). We are spiritual mentors, coaches, teachers, mothers, and fathers in the faith.

We must surround ourselves with the right friends to make the right decisions and do the right thing, the good works that glorify God.

Blessed is the man
who does not walk in the counsel of the wicked
or stand in the way of sinners
or sit in the seat of mockers.
(Ps. 1:1)

-8-

Change Demands Faith, Hope, and Love.

We are empowered by God's Spirit with three irrepressible forces of change—faith, hope, and love. Each of these provides us with the motivation, courage, and strength to press forward and not quit to make a difference in our families, church, and community.

> *And so **faith, hope, love** abide [**faith**--conviction and belief respecting man's relation to God and divine things; **hope**-- joyful and confident expectation of eternal salvation; **love**- -true affection for God and man, growing out of God's love for and in us], these three; but the greatest of these is love.* (1 Cor. 13:13)

-9-

***Change* Pushes Us Into God's Presence and Ceaseless Prayer.**

The Greek definition for *substance* is "that upon which we stand." Of course, the solid foundation for change is Christ Himself, and He is our rock and refuge in the storms and crises that plague us in life.

Change is becoming more like Christ, being conformed and transformed by His image.

> *Now the Lord is that Spirit: and where the Spirit of the Lord is, there is liberty. But we all, with open face beholding as in a glass the glory of the Lord,*

*are **changed** into the same image from glory to glory,*
even as by the Spirit of the Lord.
(2 Cor. 3:17-18)

-10-

***Change* Starts NOW!**

"Watch for the Change, I [the Lord] am doing it Now!"
(Isa. 43:19)

Stop procrastinating.
    Don't be afraid.
        Refuse to be distracted.
            Decide to trust and obey God.
                Focus ... Fight ... Finish Strong.
                    Be Confident, Committed, and Courageous.

Don't listen to the lies of the Enemy when he tells you there's ...

➢ Not enough money & resources
➢ No one to help you or you are all alone
➢ Not enough time
➢ Not the right person–you are damaged goods
➢ If you change, it won't make a difference anyway.

Get the *FUD* out of your life: Get the *Fear, Uncertainty,* and *Doubt* out of you.

Be confident in the Lord as you change because you have ...

- NOTHING TO LOSE
- NOTHING TO HIDE
- NOTHING TO FEAR

For the LORD will be your confidence, And will keep your foot from being caught [snared]. (Pro. 3:26)

*Therefore do not cast away your confidence, which has great reward. (*Heb. 10:35)

It is better to trust in the LORD
Than to put confidence in man.
It is better to trust in the LORD
Than to put confidence in princes.
(Ps. 118:8-9)

Chapter 8

Pastoring From a Distance, Where Do We Go from Here?

Where there is no vision,
the people perish.
(Pro. 29:18)

The book of Proverbs is one of the most practical books in the Old Testament. Reading the writings in Proverbs from King Solomon gives correction, warning, and encouragement. Like the author of Proverbs, I want to encourage all pastors and parishioners to not only have a vision, but to be supportive of the vision. The vision that is given to the pastor is given from God.

The vision is God's plan for His people. God's plan for His people keeps them from wandering in darkness. Solomon makes it clear in this Proverb when he writes that without the vision, we are left to wander in the dark down a path that ultimately leads to destruction. Churches that are closing and ministries that are dying are the result of not having a vision and thus journeying down a dark path of destruction. Scripture teaches us that God spoke through the prophets to communicate His plans for His people.

If you want to be a ministry that survives these chaotic times, then having a vision that exceeds being inside of the church is essential. To be impactful, your vision must include your church, community, and culture. These are the areas that the pastor must keep in mind when casting their vision. To execute the vision that God has placed upon the pastor, a Spirit filled team led by God must be formed to carry out the mandate. This ministry team should have the characteristics of being supportive, stable, and strong.

Our ministry wouldn't have lasted thus far if we didn't have a team of strong, stable, and supportive people. If you have a team right now that's not being proactive and productive, then it's time to establish a new team. I found out that there are people that want to leave a ministry, or many are there because the pastor asked them. A person's heart must be connected first to God and then to the duty and responsibility of the vision. You will know if their heart isn't in because their actions and deeds will show.

So, pastor partner with your community. Community partner with your pastor, and together you can make a change. Here is what I challenge for both the pulpit and the pew: Be the change you want to see in your church and in your community. Let it first start with you.

About The Author

Dr. Jesse E. Thomas believes in empowering the church of today for a better tomorrow and equipping them with the knowledge of Christ. He serves as the Senior Pastor of the Shiloh Baptist Church of Boston, VA, the ministry that is Encouraging, Empowering, and Edifying Disciples. Pastor Jesse Thomas is the founder and servant leader of the Impact United Fellowship. Rev. Thomas is also the author of *No More Distractions* and *Release Your Past*.

Dr. Thomas has a yearning for knowledge which has enabled him to earn a Diploma of Ministry, an Associate of Ministry, and a Bachelor of Christian Ministry from the Chesapeake Bible College & Seminary. In addition, Dr. Thomas is an Alumnus of the Chesapeake Bible College & Seminary Alumni Association. He received his Master of Divinity degree and earned his Doctor of Ministry degree from Virginia University of Lynchburg.

Pastor Jesse E. Thomas is a treasure to the body of Christ. He is a dedicated member of NAACP and a member of the United National Free Mason, in which he is the Chaplain for the state of Maryland.

He is the proud husband of Mrs. Tina Thomas and a devoted father to Jessiah and Jessica–his miracle babies, both weighing nearly 1.5 lbs. at their birth. He strongly believes in leading his family by consistently exercising his faith in God. For this reason, he lives by Romans 8:28: "And we know that in all things God works for the good of those who love him, who have been called according to his purpose."

Dr. Jesse E. Thomas
P.O. Box 4301
Salisbury, MD. 21803
www.Shilohbaptistva.org
1(800)457-2392

Printed in the USA
CPSIA information can be obtained
at www.ICGtesting.com
LVHW021937091123
763520LV00055B/1208